Dogs

LEVEL 1

/d/g/
/o/c/

DEC🐸DABLES BY jump!

Teaching Tips

Pink Level 1

This book focuses on the phonemes **/d/g/o/c/**.

Before Reading

- Discuss the title. Ask readers what they think the book will be about.
- Sound out the words on page 3 together.

Read the Book

- Ask readers to use a finger to follow along with each word as it is read.
- Encourage readers to break down unfamiliar words into units of sound. Then, ask them to string the sounds together to create the words.
- Urge readers to point out when the focused phonics phonemes appear in the text.

After Reading

- Encourage children to reread the book independently or with a friend.
- Ask simple questions about the text to check for understanding. Have them find the pages that have the answers to your questions.

© 2024 Booklife Publishing
This edition is published by arrangement with Booklife Publishing.

North American adaptations © 2024 Jump!
5357 Penn Avenue South
Minneapolis, MN 55419
www.jumplibrary.com

Decodables by Jump! are published by Jump! Library.
All rights reserved. No part of this book may be reproduced in any form without written permission from the publisher.

Library of Congress Cataloging-in-Publication Data is available at www.loc.gov or upon request from the publisher.

ISBN: 979-8-88996-765-1 (hardcover)
ISBN: 979-8-88996-766-8 (paperback)
ISBN: 979-8-88996-767-5 (ebook)

Photo Credits
Images are courtesy of Shutterstock.com. With thanks to Getty Images, Thinkstock Photo and iStockphoto. Cover – Eric Isselee. 4–5 – MaraZe, Tara Lynn and Co. 6–7 – Eric Isselee, Ermolaev Alexander. 8–9 – Ksenia Raykova. 10–11 – ANURAK PONGPATIMET, Martin Valigursky. 15 – Shutterstock.

Can you find these words in the book?

can

dog

got

hug

It is a dog.

Sip, sip, sip.

I can pat a dog.

Pat, pat, pat.

Run to get it.

The dog got it.

A dog is fun.

I can hug the dog.

Can you say these sounds and draw them with your finger?

Using the Letter Bank, trace the
missing letter into each word.

__an

__og

hu__

g__t

Letter Bank

d   o   g   c

What other words do you know
with the letters /d/, /g/, /o/, or /c/?

goat

hog

dig

Practice reading the book again:

It is a dog.

Sip, sip, sip.

I can pat a dog.

Pat, pat, pat.

Run to get it.

The dog got it.

A dog is fun.

I can hug the dog.